A Guide for Parents and Teachers

The TOOLIEZ Tool-Rific™ CLUB

WORKBOOK

Character Building Tools & Life Skill Lessons

For Ages 9-12

The TOOLIEZ TOOLBOX

By Alonzo Herro

Your Guide To Becoming A Capable, Confident and Independent Twee

Copyright

> Special imprints, messages, and excerpts can be produced to meet your needs. For more information, contact us.

E-mail: info@tooliezworld.com

This Book Belongs To:

_____

Hello Tool-Mate!

If you are a tween or teenager who is excited to become a productive and responsible citizen, then please keep reading! You will discover character building tools and life skill lessons that will help you to be better prepared for your teen and adult life. As you become more independent, you will be able to help your parents, build self-esteem and function on your own. Our goal is to prepare you for life beyond high school and college.

I, _____, agree to follow the rules set by my parents and teachers and to do my best to complete all the exercises in this workbook. I promise to honor God, dream big, study hard, work smart and be the best version of myself. I make this promise under my own free will. I agree to practice the values of The Tooliez so that I can become a member of The Tooliez Tool-Rific Club.

Member Signature_____ Date _____

Parent/Teacher Signature _____ Date_____

The Philosophy

Dear Parent/Teacher:

The Tooliez books are specifically designed to provide new and creative ways to help build your child's mind, body and spirit. Our goal is to promote character building and life skill lessons for children so that they may have better relationships with family and friends and uphold good moral standards.

Tooliez World LLC seeks to reinforce The Tooliez seven tools of character: discipline, honesty, respect, confidence, wisdom, humility, and creativity. The Tooliez workbook provides easy and fun fill-ins, quick quizzes, wonderful word projects, and creative sound suggestions.

We encourage you and your preteen to explore these exercises together. We believe that the skills taught in this book will help your child to discover more about him/herself, and you will learn more about your child. The skills will also help children to live a positive and productive life.

Having great character helps children to be kinder, make better choices and develop integrity, self-discipline and responsibility. People with good character try to make choices that are "right" and avoid behaving in a way that society considers to be "wrong". "Good" morals or values are generally accepted as being "right" choices, like being honest, respectful, responsible and caring. These qualities are necessary to be contributors to society which is the goal of character education when taught to children.

Tooliez World's goal is to promote Tool-Rific kidz. Nice kidz are nice, good kidz are good, but Tool-Rific kidz are Tool-Rificly well-rounded!

TOOL-RIFIC stands for **T**alented, **O**ptimistic, **O**bedient, **L**oyal, **R**espectful, **I**nquisitive, **F**riendly, **I**ndependent and **C**ourageous.

The Tooliez Tool-Rific Workbook

Character Building Tools & Life Skill Lessons

TABLE of CONTENTS

All About Me!

Please complete this form and record important facts about yourself. This form will help you learn more about yourself and help your parents learn more about you.
No one knows you better than you do.

FACTS ABOUT ME

Name _____ Age ____ Race _____ M __ F__

Address _____ City _____ State _____

School _____ Grade _____ Teacher _____

Favorite Subject _____ Least Favorite Subject _____

Sport/Hobby _____ Clubs _____

Favorite: Relative_____ Friend_____

Favorite: Color_____ Food _____ Fruit _____

Book _____ Movie/Show _____ Game _____

Music _____ Pastime _____ Vacation_____

Are you or do you know someone who is being bullied? Yes _____ No_____

MEMBERS OF MY FAMILY

_____

Which family member do you like most?_____ least?_____

Why? _____

If you can change one thing in your life, what would it be?_____

I BELIEVE

On a scale of 1-10, how much do you believe these statements to be true?

1 (Low)	2	3	4	5	6	7	8	9	10 (High)

I believe that I will be happy and successful in life _____

I believe that I am a kind and considerate person _____

I believe that I am a positive role model for others _____

I believe that I have a bright future ahead of me _____

I believe that I am funny and have a great sense of humor _____

I believe that I am smart _____

I believe that I have a positive impact on others _____

I believe that my friends care for me and support me _____

I believe that I am a good friend _____

I believe that I am special and unique _____

I believe that I am an important member of my family _____

I believe that I am talented _____

I believe that I have the power to be who I want to be in life _____

I believe that I can overcome any challenge that I face _____

I believe that my goals are achievable _____

I believe that my thoughts, feelings and words are important _____

I believe that I have the power to change the world _____

I believe that I am going to accomplish great things in life _____

I believe that my views and opinions matter and should be heard _____

I believe that I am someone who is fun to be around _____

I believe that I make smart decisions _____

I believe that I am in control of my emotions _____

CTRL+ALT+DEL

Control yourself
Alter your thinking
Delete negativity

The TOOLIEZ ™

The **Tooliez** are a fictional team of seven Tool-Rific Action Heroes who are part human and part tool, each with a unique superpower. Together, the team must harness their new special abilities to help children unleash their inner **POWER** and fight the influence of negative human behavior. **TOOLIEZ** is an acronym for Tools Open Opportunities so Learning **Is EZ**.

Their mission is to provide parents and teachers the necessary tools to help encourage, equip and empower every kid to be a Tool-Rific **HERO** - **H**elp **E**ncourage & **R**each **O**thers!

Meet The Tooliez and Discover their Tool-Rific Powers

SGT. Drill Bit the Drill, Leader of The Tooliez and an Army Airborne Ranger. He represents the Tool of **Discipline** (obedience and self-control). He is highly motivated, disciplined, organized and tough. He loves to maintain order and to help others solve their problems. He enjoys practicing karate and playing basketball. His favorite color is green and his favorite food is double cheeseburger. **Superpowers**: He has superhuman strength, speed, durability, agility, and stamina. He has the power to regenerate himself if wounded, and the power to propel energy beams through his special gloves. He is able to fly using his magical backpack, which can transform into anything, and he wears a utility belt loaded with secret gadgets.

Hammie the Hammer, a Lawyer. She represents the Tool of **Honesty** (truth and righteousness). She is seriously focused and believes in obeying the law and doing the right thing at all times. She enjoys dancing and playing board games. Her favorite color is pink and her favorite food is hot dogs. **Superpowers:** She can communicate with people telepathically, manipulate their minds, and influence their decisions to do what's right. She also has a special hammer that can create an explosive shock wave to knock things down, and a force field to protect herself from attacks.

Cutter the Saw, a Surgeon. He represents the Tool of **Respect** (honor, admiration and reverence). He strongly believes in giving respect to all people (especially those in authority), their property and culture. He enjoys running and wood carving. His favorite color is blue and his favorite food is cheesy pizza. **Superpowers:** He has the power to run at the speed of light and is able to cut through anything with his blades of steel.

Screwee the Screwdriver, an Entertainer. He represents the Tool of **Confidence** (assurance and self-belief). He is funny, silly, and energetic. He has a dual personality: either calm and focused or wild and misbehaved. He enjoys acting and tumbling. His favorite color is orange and his favorite food is spiral fries. **Superpowers:** He has the power to spin to create a tornado, pull things into his vortex, and then shoot them out to wherever he desires. He is able to fly and perform other wind-related feats.

Ruly the Ruler, a Professor. He represents the Tool of **Wisdom** (intelligence and knowledge). He is smart, accurate, intelligent and sophisticated. He is a member of Mensa and enjoys reading, writing and mathematics. His favorite color is red and his favorite food is ravioli with meat sauce. **Superpowers:** He has the power of super intelligence and is able to think faster and answer questions more accurately than anyone. He also has the power of elasticity and can stretch his body to unbelievable lengths and shapes at will.

Gripper the Wrench, a Construction Engineer. He represents the Tool of **Humility** (meek and peaceful). He is strong, shy, quiet, and humble. Connecting things is his specialty. He enjoys swimming and weight lifting. His favorite color is golden yellow and his favorite food is a grilled chicken sandwich. **Superpowers:** He possesses tremendous superhuman strength, durability, and endurance. He can double his strength and size by turning the screw mechanism on the sides of his head.

Beutie the Paintbrush, an Artist. She represents the Tool of **Creativity** (artistic and inventive). She is glamorous, conceited and proud. She looks for the best in everything. She enjoys drawing, painting and decorating. Her favorite color is purple and her favorite food is baked goods. **Superpowers:** She has the power to camouflage herself in any surrounding, paint pictures that come alive, repair anything that is broken and teleport herself and others in and out of her paintings.

Now that you have learned about The Tooliez character traits and powers, it's your turn to discover your super abilities to become a Hero at home, in school and in your community.

Part One:

Building

Character

Good Character Education

Good character education can provide ground rules for life. It is crucial for tweens to develop good character so that they can be mentally equipped to make wise, moral decisions and overcome any obstacles in life. They will not only lead happier lives, but they will also lead more successful lives.

"Good character is not formed in a week or a month. It is created little by little, day by day. Protracted and patient effort is needed to develop good character."

Heraclitus of Ephesus

"Watch your thoughts; they become words.

Watch your words; they become actions.

Watch your actions; they become habit.

Watch your habits; they become character.

Watch your character; it becomes your destiny."

Lao Tzu

The Importance of Character

A person with good character is someone whose actions reflect one's beliefs, and those beliefs are based on strong principles such as integrity, honesty, respect, responsibility, care, and other "good" traits.

Learning about good character is a critical part of education and stresses the importance of helping children to practice behaviors that reflect universal, ethical values. Character education helps children and youth to become conscious of the right thing to do.

Teachers and parents talk about having and building good character and good character traits, but what does this all mean? A person's character is shown by how they act, think and feel in life. Character is not one thing; it is a combination of how someone interacts with others and what they think of themselves. Good traits, also referred to as good values or good morals, represent qualities that society generally agrees will help people to do well in life.

Study the Meaning of The Seven Tools of Character

Discipline – Honor Your Faith, Family and Country. Obedience and self-control. Listen to your parents and leaders, follow instructions, push yourself against your will to accomplish your goals, finish what you start, do what you are supposed to do, persevere and keep trying, do your best, use self-control, be self-disciplined, think before you act, consider the consequences of your actions, be accountable for your choices.

Honesty – Be truthful and upright. Truth and justice. Be true to yourself and others, be forthcoming and upright, do not lie, steal, cheat, deceive or cut corners in order to win or gain in life, be reliable, do what you say you will do, build a good reputation, do the right thing, be loyal, stand by your family, friends and community.

Respect – Appreciate your parents, leaders, teachers and all humanity, animals, nature and property. Admiration and appreciation. Strive to practice good manners, be tolerant of differences, be considerate of other people's property and living creatures, treat others as you want them to treat you, follow the golden rules, do not use inappropriate language, be considerate of others' feelings, don't tease, threaten, hit or hurt anyone, deal peacefully with anger, insults and disagreements.

Confidence – Believe in yourself, be brave, assertive and ready to challenge your mental and physical fears. Assurance and self-belief. Say and do what you feel is right, be willing to take a stand for your beliefs, be aggressive and bold, be prepared, take charge of your life, go for the goal, choose wisely, challenge yourself to lead.

Wisdom – Demonstrate good judgment, strive to go above and beyond, learn not to settle. Intelligent and knowledgeable. Demonstrate good judgment, don't settle for less, get what you deserve, feel free to ask questions, try to go above and beyond your grade level, study hard, ask tough questions, do the homework.

Humility – Agree to take the high road, never abuse your power and volunteer to assist others in need. Meek and peaceful. Be compassionate, don't take advantage of others, play by the rules, take turns and share, be open-minded, listen to others, don't blame others for your actions, be kind and show that you care, express gratitude, forgive others, help people in need.

Creativity – To continuously seek, practice and develop your talents. Artistic and inventive. Use your God-given talent to benefit your life and others, try new experiences, share ideas, explore your talents, make things happen, be adventurous, use your imagination.

Apply The Seven Tools of Character to your Life

DISCIPLINE HONESTY RESPECT CONFIDENCE WISDOM HUMILITY CREATIVITY

1, Discipline - _____

_____

2. Honesty - _____

_____

3, Respect - _____

_____

4, Confidence - _____

_____

5. Wisdom - _____

_____

6, Humility - _____

_____

7. Creativity - _____

_____

Practice The Seven Character Concepts

The Drill represents repetition. One must study or practice a skill over and over again in order to become very good at it. **This is the character of Discipline -** obedience and self-control - always listen to your leaders and follow instructions, push yourself against your will to accomplish your goals, finish what you start.

The Hammer stands for accuracy. One must stay focused and not deviate from being good. **This is the character of Honesty** - truth and justice - always be true to yourself and others, be forthcoming and upright, do not lie, steal, cheat or cut corners in order to win or gain in life.

The Saw signifies danger. Strive to be sharp and positive, cut out negativity in your life that can prevent you from being a better person. **This is the character of Respect** - admiration and appreciation - strive to practice good manners, tolerate differences, be considerate of other people's property, nature, animals and living creatures.

The Screwdriver symbolizes insecurity. The do's and don'ts of life. You must take a stand for the values that you believe in, even when others have different beliefs or values. **This is the character of Confidence** - assurance and self-belief - believe in yourself, be willing to be bold and aggressive, challenge your mental and physical fears.

The Ruler stands for expansion. You must study and work hard to acquire as much knowledge as you can to achieve your goals. Dream big and reach for the stars. **This is the character of Wisdom** - intelligence and knowledge - demonstrate good judgment, never settle, get what you deserve, feel free to ask questions, always try to go above and beyond your grade level.

The Wrench represents connection. You can't achieve much by yourself, but you can accomplish more when you team up with others. **This is the character of Humility -** meekness and peace - be compassionate, don't take advantage of others, take the high road, never abuse your power, help people in need.

The Paintbrush symbolizes renewal and rejuvenation. Don't allow dark situations to stop you from seeing the bright side of life. **This is the character of Creativity** - artistic and inventive - use your God-given talent to make things better for yourself and others.

How to use The Seven Tools of Character Concepts in your Life

DRILL   HAMMER   SAW   SCREWDRIVER   RULER   WRENCH   PAINTBRUSH

1. The Drill will help me _____

_____

2. The Hammer will help me _____

_____

3. The Saw will help me _____

_____

4. The Screwdriver will help me _____

_____

5. The Ruler will help me _____

_____

6. The Wrench will help me _____

_____

7. The Paintbrush will help me _____

_____

CHARACTER

"Be more concerned with your character than your reputation, because your character is what you really are, while your reputation is merely what others think you are."

John Wooden

Part Two

ASSESS YOURSELF!

"There is no greater delight than to be conscious of sincerity on self-examination."
Mencius

Self-Awareness

Self-awareness is the knowledge of self in three basic areas: **cognitive, physical and emotional.** It is the ability to recognize your own feelings, behaviors, and characteristics. Being self-aware can help you take better care of yourself, have deeper relationships, and live a more fulfilling life.

What causes lack of self-awareness? People who are not self-aware are afraid to be vulnerable. They are worried that they will be judged or rejected by others, which causes them to be unaware of their feelings, thoughts, motives, and behaviors.

Five ways to increase your self-awareness:

1. Practice mindfulness and meditation. Mindfulness is being present in the moment and paying attention to yourself and your surroundings rather than getting lost in thought or daydreaming.
2. Practice yoga
3. Make time to reflect
4. Journal
5. Ask the opinion of people you love

Self-Awareness Worksheet

Emotions usually affect the actions of a person.
Given the following situations, what would you do?

You see an old man crossing the street so you

_____
_____
_____
_____

You and your friend had a fight. You would

_____
_____
_____
_____

Your mom refuses to buy something you really want. How would you feel and what would you do?

_____
_____
_____

Someone says bad things about you behind your back. How would you feel and what would you do?

_____
_____
_____
_____

Self-Assessment

Self-assessment- the act or process of analyzing and evaluating oneself or one's actions and attitudes, for example, of one's performance on a job

How does self-assessment work? A self-assessment is a process through which you can learn more about yourself, rate your performance and identify developmental needs. You can perform self-assessments on a variety of areas, including personal development, skills and relationships.

Why does self-assessment work? Recognizing your strengths and weaknesses will help you to make better choices for yourself and boost your self-confidence.

What are self-assessment questions? Self-evaluation questions are specifically designed to help you review your own performance in school and at work. These questions are designed to promote reflection and encourage teens to spend time thinking about what they want to accomplish in life.

Self-Assessment Worksheet

NAME _____	Always	Sometimes	Rarely
I listen when my parent or teacher is talking			
I follow instructions the first time they are given			
I am polite and respectful to students and adults			
I raise my hand to answer questions in class			
I take my time and do my BEST work			
My handwriting and work are NEAT			
I finish my work ON TIME			
I am kind to other students at school			
I walk quietly in the hallways			
I keep things organized in my desk			
I am prepared to learn everyday			
I ask for help when I need it			
I have a positive attitude at home and school			
I socialize in class when I should pay attention to teacher			
I complete my homework and chores			

How do you feel about life at home? _____

WHY? _____

How do you feel about school? _____

WHY? _____

Write about something you would like to improve: _____

WHY? _____

Write about an area you do well: _____

Page 21

Finding Yourself

What does it mean to find yourself?

When you find yourself, you can live authentically and be true to who you are at your core. This means embracing your strengths, accepting your weaknesses, and showing up in the world as your genuine self. Living the best version of yourself allows you to attract people and experiences that align with your true essence.

DISCOVERING YOUR PURPOSE IN LIFE

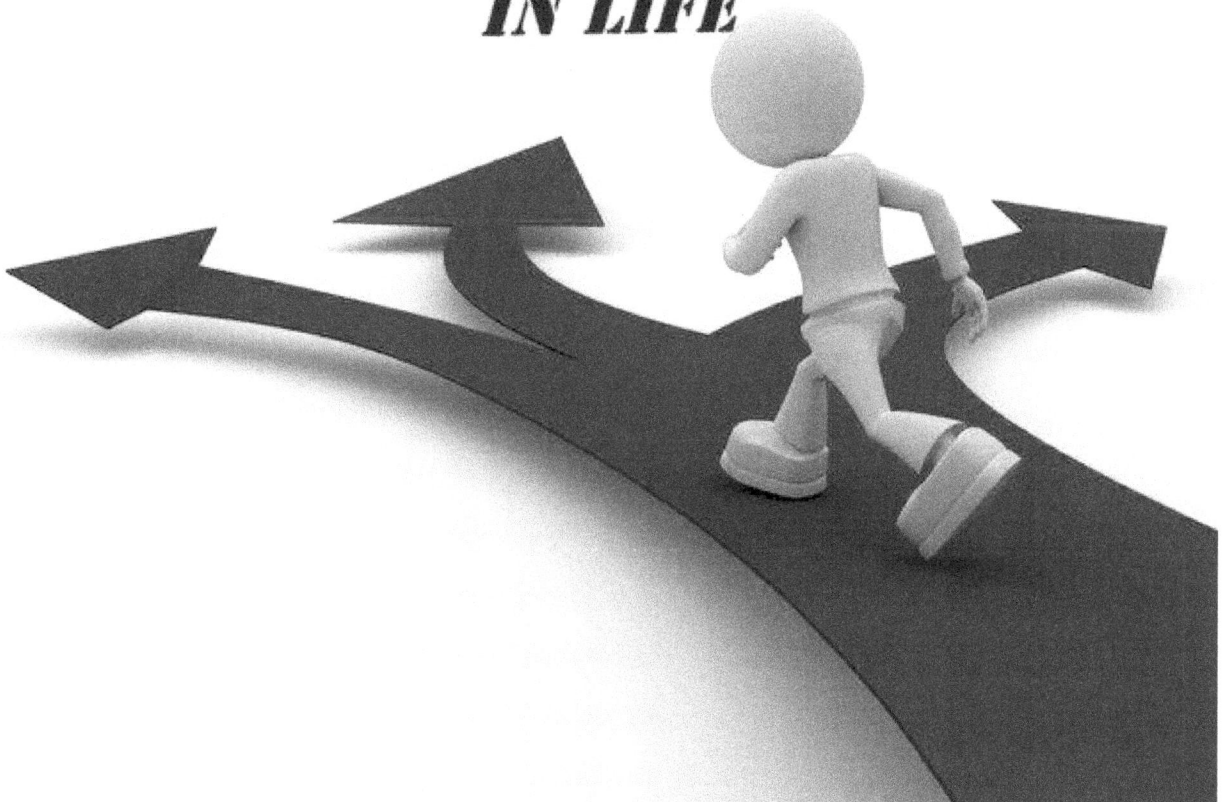

Discovering your Purpose
What is your purpose?

Finding yourself helps you uncover your purpose in life. By understanding your values, passions and unique gifts, you can identify the path that will give you the most fulfillment and meaning. Your purpose gives you a sense of direction and guides your decisions, leading to a more purposeful and satisfying life.

Eight tips to help you get acquainted with yourself

1. Visualize your ideal lifestyle

2. Reflect on your relationships

3. Do things on your own

4. Focus on your passions

5. Keep yourself organized

6. Know your triggers and when to unplug

7. Learn the difference between support and opinions

8. Make a list of things you value

Self-Love

Accept your emotions for what they are and put your physical, emotional and mental well-being first

Self-love is a state of appreciation for oneself that grows from actions that support physical, psychological and spiritual growth. Self-love means having a high regard for your own well-being and happiness. Self-love means taking care of your own needs and not sacrificing your well-being to please others.

What are the 4 types of self-love?

Self-awareness, Self-worth, Self-esteem, Self-care

If any of these is missing, then you do not entirely have self-love. You should be aligned with these four types. The journey of achieving self-love does not differ from confronting your demons which is the reason most of us lack it. Having an honest conversation with yourself is not easy. Self-love is hard to achieve because it means having to do away with certain things and people you like to be around. Our addiction to people and habits that go against the premise of self-love means that we compromise and love ourselves conditionally, in exchange for the momentary rush we get from these distractions.

How do you show self-love?

1. Replace criticism and comparison with acceptance and appreciation
2. Communicate with yourself in kind and positive ways
3. Show respect for yourself by setting boundaries and prioritizing your needs
4. Spend quality time by yourself
5. Develop trust in yourself by honoring your commitments

Managing Emotions

Emotion - A natural, instinctive state of mind deriving from one's circumstances, moods, or relationships with others

Some emotions are positive: happiness, joy, interest, excitement, gratitude, and love. These positive emotions make a person feel good. Negative emotions – sadness, anger, loneliness, jealousy, self-criticism, fear, or rejection – can even be painful at times. This is especially true when we feel a negative emotion strongly or too often, or dwell on it for too long. Negative emotions may be difficult, but we can learn to handle them.

Here are 3 steps that can help manage emotions.

Step 1: Identify the Emotion – Learning to notice and identify your feelings takes practice. In addition to focusing on your feelings, check in with your body too. You may feel sensations with certain emotions - perhaps your face gets hot or your muscles tense.

- **Be aware of how you feel**. When you have a negative emotion such as anger, identify what you're feeling rather than pretend not to have the feeling at all or lose your temper.
- **Figure out what caused the feeling.** Understanding the source of your feelings will help you to figure out the best way to handle them.
- **Don't blame.** Recognizing or explaining your emotion is not the same as blaming someone or something for the way you feel. Your feelings will help you make sense of what is going on.
- **Accept your emotions as natural and understandable.** Don't judge yourself for the emotions you feel. Accept how you feel as normal and don't be hard on yourself.

Step 2: Take Action – Once you have identified and understood what you are feeling, you can decide how to express your emotions. Sometimes it's enough to process how you feel in your head, but other times you'll want to do something to feel better.

- **Think about the best way to express your emotions.** Do you need to gently confront someone else, talk things over with a friend or work off the feelings by going for a run?
- **Learn how to change your mood.** Try doing activities that make you happy, even if you don't feel like it at the time.
- **Build positive emotions.** Focus on what is good in your life, even the little things such as a parent praising you for fixing the Wi-Fi or for making a delicious salad. Noticing the good things, even when you're feeling down, can help you shift emotional balance from negative to positive.
- **Find support.** Talk about your feelings with a parent, other trusted adult or friend. This can help you explore your emotions and give you a fresh way of thinking.
- **Exercise.** Physical activity helps the brain make natural chemicals that can boost your mood. Exercise can also release stress and help prevent you from focusing on negative feelings.

Step 3: Seek Help for Difficult Emotions – Sometimes, no matter what you do, you can't shake a tough emotion. If you have feelings of sadness or worry for more than a day, or if you feel so upset that you think you might hurt yourself or other people, you need to seek help immediately. Speak with a trusted adult (parent, school counselor, teacher or coach) right away. If you don't have an adult you can turn to, reach out to someone on a helpline. There are people to talk to 24/7. They can listen and guide you on how to get the help you need.

In the United States, one resource is Substance Abuse and Mental Health Services Administration (SAMHSA). Call 1-800-662-HELP (4357) or text your zip code to 435748 (HELP4U) to find help near you.

Managing Emotions Worksheet
Exploring My Feelings

The Situation _____

Identify four feelings you are experiencing about the situation

1	2	3	4

1. I feel _____ because _____

_____

2. I feel _____ because _____

_____

3. I feel _____ because _____

_____

4. I feel _____ because _____

_____

What can you do to cope with these feelings?

_____

_____

Aggression

The act of attacking without provocation

Aggression is any behavior, verbal or physical, that involves attacking another person, animal or object with the intention of harming the target. Similarly, violence is intentionally using physical force to hurt or damage someone or something.

What does it mean to be aggressive? Aggressive behavior involves showing anger and/or a willingness to attack other people. For example, when someone who is criticized gets aggressive and starts shouting.

What does an aggressive person do?

Aggression, according to social psychology, describes any behavior or act aimed at harming a person or animal or damaging physical property. A few examples of aggressive acts are physical violence, shouting, swearing, and harsh language.

What are the 3 types of aggression?

The three aggression types are **reactive-expressive** (i.e. verbal and physical), **reactive-inexpressive** (i.e. hostility), and **proactive-relational aggression** (i.e. when relationships are broken, for instance, by circulating malicious rumors).

Aggressive: Forceful and direct, quick to act. Aggressive behavior can have positive results but they are often negative.

Passive: Not active, not responsive, not showing resistance.

Why do people get aggressive?

The environment can contribute to aggression on many levels. Interpersonal, social, group, neighborhood, economic and cultural conditions can create the potential for aggression. In social situations, frustrations can accumulate over time which is referred to as an incubation period.

What are some early signs of an aggressive person?

- Anxiety
- Moodiness
- Agitation, constant irritability
- Easily angered
- Disorientation or memory problem
- Depression or flat affect
- Trouble with concentration and attention
- Trouble thinking in an organized manner
- Poor communication skills, overt negative affect

Aggression Worksheet

1. Do you think people are born aggressive? Why or why not? Does it matter if they are? _____

_____

_____

2. Do you think harmful aggression is learned or do you think people are born that way? Why? _____

_____

3. Where and how do you think people learn harmful, aggressive behavior? _____

_____

4. Are people ever rewarded for positive aggressive behavior? _____

What would those behaviors be? _____

_____

5. What rewards are given for acting in a positive, aggressive way? _____

_____

Emotional Triggers

Emotional triggers are automatic responses to the way people express anger, sadness or other emotions.

Emotional triggers, also called mental health triggers or psychological triggers, are memories, objects or people that spark intense, negative emotions. This change in emotions can be abrupt, and in many cases, will cause a response that is more severe than necessary. Find a way to recognize these feelings and calm yourself.

clicking

chewing

swallowing

barking

whistling

What are causes of emotional triggers in life?

Common triggers that create an emotional response could result from hearing a certain song, being in an unsafe environment, or remembering a traumatic event.

For example, when someone is asked to make a presentation at work, an emotional trigger to public speaking could involve symptoms such as:

Dizziness, Chest pain, Rapid heart rate, Nausea, Shaking, Anger, Anxiety, Sadness

Depending on which symptoms the individual feels, he/she may have one of several mental health triggers.

Other reasons that people suffer from emotional triggers:

1. Someone leaving you (or the threat that they will), for example, in death or a relationship breakup

2. Helplessness over painful situations

3. Ignored or disregarded by someone

Eight Strategies to Help you Identify, Manage and Heal Emotional Triggers

1. Identify your top three triggers

2. Understand what happens right before a reaction

3. Tell your story

4. Recognize the physical signs

5. Find an effective method to interrupt your reaction

6. Take deep breaths

7. Change the atmosphere

8. Practice thought-stopping

What is a common method of managing emotions after they have been triggered?

- Step 1: Pause - Instead of acting on a feeling right away, stop before reacting too quickly.
- Step 2: Acknowledge your feelings - Are you mad at someone or are you sad because your feelings were hurt by what they did or said?
- Step 3: Think – How should you handle the situation and move forward?
- Step 4: Seek help or counseling if needed

Identify Your Triggers Worksheet

How likely is it that a potential trigger would make you mad?

Trigger	Not at all	Very little	Somewhat	Definitely
Someone hits me by mistake				
Someone hits me on purpose				
Someone talks about me behind my back				
Someone says something mean to me				
My parent yells at me for something I did				
A teacher yells at me for something I did				
Someone interrupts me while talking				
Someone lies on me				
Someone touches my belongings				
I can't find something I need				
Someone's not in line				
I lose in a game				
My friend didn't call me back				

Anger Management

Control anger before it controls you

Anger management – The goal of anger management is to reduce your emotional feelings and the physiological arousal that anger causes.

Why do I get angry so easily?

What causes anger issues? Many things can trigger anger, including stress, family problems and financial issues. For some people, anger is caused by an underlying disorder, such as alcoholism or depression. Anger itself isn't considered a disorder, but anger is a known symptom of several mental health conditions.

What is the best way to control your anger?

1. Count to 10. Give yourself time to cool down so you can think more clearly and overcome the impulse to lash out.

2. Breathe slowly

3. Exercise

4. Consider the consequences of your actions

5. Get creative

6. Talk about how you feel

Anger Management Worksheet

Answer the questions below to understand how well you manage your anger. For each skill, rate yourself: <u>S</u> for <u>**Strength**</u>, <u>O</u> for <u>**Okay**</u> or <u>N</u> for <u>**Needs Work**</u>

____ I am a forgiving person

____ I don't get angry very often

____ I don't get angry very easily

____ I get over my anger quickly

____ I avoid arguments with others

____ I speak positive words when I am angry

____ Little things don't bother me much

____ I rarely or never raise my voice in anger

____ I have a positive attitude towards others

____ I have a positive attitude about myself

____ I never get in trouble at school due to my anger

____ I avoid saying mean things to others when I am upset

____ I use calm down strategies or coping skills when I am angry

____ I manage my impulses and make good decisions when I am angry

____ I avoid arguing with others when I am frustrated

____ My anger does not impact my relationships with family and friends

____ I accept help from others when I am angry

____ I never slam doors, throw things, or get aggressive when I am mad

____ I never have conflicts with my family or get in trouble at home due to anger

____ I try to resolve problems before I get angry

If you can improve two areas above, which two improvements would have the greatest impact on your life?

Peer Pressure

Peer pressure involves people within a group who influence others in the same group to engage in a behavior or activity that they may not otherwise engage in. A peer can be any individual who belongs to the same social group or circle as you and who has some type of influence over you.

Here are the Six Types of Peer Pressure:

- **Spoken Peer Pressure** – A teenager asks, suggests, persuades or directs another person to engage in a specific behavior.

- **Unspoken Peer Pressure** - A teenager is exposed to the actions of one or more peers and must decide whether or not to follow along. This could take the form of fashion choices, personal interactions or decisions to join particular clubs, cliques or teams.

- **Direct Peer Pressure** - When a group clearly instructs a person on what to do or how to act. Examples include handing a person an alcoholic drink and telling them to drink it or asking a peer for every answer to a homework assignment.

- **Indirect Peer Pressure** – Instead of specific targeting of individuals, a person's behavior is influenced by the surrounding environment. For instance, at a party where there is alcohol consumption, individuals may feel compelled to drink even without an explicit invitation to do so.

- **Negative Peer Pressure** - When a friend or someone who is part of a group you belong to makes you feel that you have to do something against your will to be accepted. It's the negative peer pressure that we usually think of when the phrase "peer pressure" is used.

- **Positive Peer Pressure** – When peers influence a person to do something positive for personal growth. For example, peers who are committed to doing well in school or sports can influence others to be more goal-oriented. Similarly, peers who are kind, loyal or supportive influence others to be the same way.

Peer Pressure Worksheet

1. Write down the names of two of your peers.

   * _____

   * _____

2. List two of your own examples of situations where you might feel pressured by your peers.

   * _____

   * _____

3. List one example of how a peer might pressure you to do something against your will.

   * _____

4. What is positive peer pressure? List one specific example.

   _____

   _____

   _____

5. What are four types of peer pressure?

   _____

   _____

Accepting Criticism

Everyone makes mistakes. It's a part of being human. When others point out our mistakes to us, it is called criticism. Some criticism is warranted and unavoidable, such as that received from a teacher in school or from a supervisor at work. Other times, criticism comes from friends, family, or even total strangers. Regardless of where it comes from, it is important to learn to see mistakes as learning opportunities and to not let criticism provoke us to react with anger. Use this worksheet to think through some criticism you have received lately.

How to gracefully accept criticism

1. Pause before reacting. When you're given criticism, the first thing you should do is pause.
2. Keep an open mind
3. Listen to understand
4. Express appreciation
5. Ask questions or for examples
6. Close the issue or ask to follow up later
7. Reframe how you think of criticism
8. Don't let it get personal

What is an example of accepting criticism? Also, highlight positive results expected if someone accepts your critique as it helps build trust and confidence _____

_____

Accepting Criticism Worksheet

Taking criticism is the ability to accept constructive feedback for improvement and to withstand the pressure of unfair or dispiriting criticisms while motivating oneself to work harder and better instead of giving up.

1. What was the criticism? _____

_____

2. Who offered the criticism? _____

_____

_____

3. Do you feel this criticism was warranted? _____

_____

4. In what way was this situation a learning opportunity?

_____

5. What will you do differently next time?

_____

Be Assertive

Having or showing a confident and forceful personality

Being assertive means communicating with others in a direct and honest manner without intentionally hurting anyone's feelings. Direct communication can reduce conflict, build self-confidence and enhance personal and work relationships. Assertiveness is a skill that anyone can learn.

What is an assertive person like? People who speak assertively send the message that they believe in themselves. They're not too timid and they're not too pushy. They know that their feelings and ideas matter. They are confident and tend to make friends easily. Being assertive shows that you respect yourself because you're willing to stand up for your interests and express your thoughts and feelings. It also demonstrates that you're aware of others' rights and willing to work on resolving conflicts.

What are the 3 C's of assertive communication? They are Confidence, Clarity and Control. **Confidence:** You believe in your ability to handle a situation. **Clarity:** Your message is easy to understand and is not exaggerated. **Control:** You remain calm while expressing yourself.

Be Assertive Worksheet

Place a checkmark next to examples of assertive communication.

Assertive communication means you stand up for yourself and share how you feel in a respectful manner.

____Chloe asks, "Can you please stop throwing the ball at me?"

____ Diane pushes Al because he called her a bad name.

____James says, "No. I don't like it when you do that."

____Chris calls Bo "chicken brain" because he's mad at him.

____Kelly never says anything when someone makes fun of her.

____Fran doesn't let Paul play her game because she's mad at him.

____Carol says, "Stop calling me names behind my back!"

____ Jack tells Brenda that she's the worst friend in the world.

____Paul pulls Eva to the side and asks her to be nicer to him.

____Sally is mad at Asher so she counts to 10 before she speaks to him.

Cultural Diversity

1. What do you know about people just by looking at them? Some people are not from the U.S. Some are Black, Asian, White or Hispanic. Some are male or female with different clothing and hairstyles.

2. By looking at others, can you tell the language they speak? Whether they are rich, poor, smart or successful? Where they live? How many people are in their family?

3. Can you determine whether or not you want to be friendly with others or not by looking at them?

4. Do you think there are people who make a judgment just by looking at a person? Do people use stereotypes to judge others? (stereotypes are judgments about an entire group of people based on opinions of a few people that are untrue)

Discrimination: An act that favors a particular person or group while putting others at a disadvantage

Prejudice: A judgment or opinion of someone without knowing anything about the person

Bigotry: A narrow-minded attitude towards certain groups of people

Racism: Any act that favors one race over another, especially when practiced by governments or large institutions

Cultural Diversity Worksheet

 A culture is a way of life of a group of people - the behaviors, beliefs, values and symbols that they accept, generally without thinking about them, and that are passed along by communication and imitation from one generation to the next. Culture is symbolic communication. Complete the boxes below with information about your culture.

Religious Beliefs:

Foods:

Holidays:

Education:

Music:

Who are you?

"How do you define who you are?" Personality traits, abilities, likes and dislikes, your belief system or moral code, and the things that motivate you - these all contribute to self-image or your unique identity as a person. People who can easily describe these aspects of their identity typically have a fairly strong sense of who they are.

When a person asks, "Who are you?" he (or she) wants to know the authentic person that embodies who you are. They are not interested in anything superficial or material.

What is the answer to "Who are you?" Begin by highlighting your current experience and achievements, then share the key skills you have developed. You may conclude by summarizing your current role and what you are seeking in your next opportunity. This method allows you to present a well-rounded answer that highlights your qualifications.

What defines who you are? A person is defined by love, resilience, self-worth, how you support and encourage other people, wisdom, current situation and faith in yourself.

How do values define who you are? Oftentimes, values guide major life decisions. Core values serve as guiding principles essential for personal development. They define the person you want to become and help you stay true to yourself. Personal values even impact how you speak and communicate.

About Me Worksheet

Name _____ Nickname _____

Age ____ Birthday _____ How many siblings? _____

Nationality _____ Religion _____

These Are My Favorite Things:

Food _____ Color _____ Snack _____

Friend _____ Music _____ Activity _____

TV Show _____ Animal _____

School Subject _____ Sports _____

What do you like to do for fun? _____

What do you struggle with? _____

_____

What would you like to learn this year?_____

How to answer "Who are you?"

1. Reflect on your experience   2. Identify your values

3. Research the company   4. Include your skills

5. Be cautious about what you share 6. Write a script

7. Practice your answer

"CREATE THE HIGHEST, GRANDEST VISION POSSIBLE

FOR YOUR LIFE,

BECAUSE YOU BECOME

WHAT YOU BELIEVE."

Oprah Winfrey

Part Three

Life Skill Lessons

Life Skills

Skills necessary or desirable for
full participation in everyday life

Life skills are a set of abilities that are necessary for success in daily life. These skills are not taught in traditional academic settings, but rather are practiced when facing the realities of life. Some development professionals believe that life skills are critical in health and social interactions.

Life skills help people make good decisions, solve problems, communicate effectively, build strong relationships and manage stress. They refer to a set of abilities that enable individuals to navigate the demands and challenges of daily life effectively.

Life skills also include behaviors that enable individuals to manage life's daily challenges and opportunities. These skills can be grouped into several categories including personal skills, social skills and practical skills. Personal skills involve self-awareness, self-management and self-motivation, while social skills involve communication, collaboration and empathy. Practical skills include problem-solving, decision-making and time management.

Life Skills to Learn

10 important life skills – Self-awareness, critical thinking, creative thinking, empathy, decision-making, problem-solving, effective communication, interpersonal relationships, coping with emotions and stress management.

Life skills that are essential tools to understand one's own strengths and weaknesses:

- Time management
- Basic money management
- How to plan and cook nutritious meals
- Giving without expectations
- How to set and hold boundaries regardless of another person's reaction
- Demonstrating positive behaviors and taking care of yourself as you become more independent
- Speaking or owning your truth without needing that truth to be validated by others
- How to check your ego and not let it drive your behavior
- How to be still in nature

What life skills do you need to work on? _____

_____

Parent Approved _____ **Teacher Approved** _____ **Total Points** _____

The Tooliez Seven Blocks of Life Skills

Family Values – These are rules, beliefs and traditions that are important to your family such as being kind, showing good manners, respecting yourself and others, sharing, spending quality time together, expressing feelings, communicating often, and forgiving each other. Family values also help you to build a strong identity and to have positive relationships.

Education – Both academics and real life experiences form the foundation of education. It is important to gain knowledge and skills in subjects such as reading, writing and math, and to study hard in school. Learn from others' experiences and mistakes so that you can have a better, well-rounded life.

Teamwork and Sportsmanship – Be a good leader and follow directions when working with others to achieve a common goal. You can interact and communicate well with others by expressing yourself in an honest and respectful way. There are winners and losers, so be a good sport no matter what the outcome.

Health, Fitness and Nutrition – It is important to take care of your body by bathing, brushing your teeth, brushing/combing your hair, taking vitamins and wearing clean clothes daily. Be careful not to spread germs to others. Your body will be strong, healthy and physically fit if you eat the right foods and exercise regularly.

Work Ethic – Learn the importance and value of hard work. Working hard will pay off with rewards of success so keep a positive attitude, make good decisions, and be responsible with money. Remember that laziness is the opposite of hard work and will not lead to a productive and joyful life.

Recreation – Leisure and recreation are what we do in our spare time or for fun, and not when we are in class, working, sleeping or taking care of responsibilities. It is free time for you to relax, read a book, work on your hobbies, participate in a sport, treat yourself to something you enjoy, or try something new.

Community Service – Volunteer to help local or national charitable organizations to benefit your community. Giving and serving others will build compassion and empathy to understand how others feel about their experiences.

Life Skills Worksheet

Dreams are what we imagine we can do in life with the belief that anything is possible, while goals are achievable targets based on your dreams and visions. Make a list of your long-term dreams and short-term goals and necessary steps to achieve them.

IMAGINE

LONG-TERM DREAMS

Imagine what your life will be like in 10-20 years. Remember that anything is possible! Write down your dreams, hopes and goals below.

1. Your long-term goal:_____

Steps to achieve goal: _____

SHORT-TERM GOALS

Based on your dreams and visions, what is a short-term goal you would like to achieve? Start with the most interesting and recent goal.

2. Your short-term goal:_____

Steps to achieve goal: _____

"Don't just dream. Make your dreams into a reality!"

Self-Esteem

Self-esteem – Confidence in one's own worth or abilities; self-respect

Self-esteem is how we value and perceive ourselves. It's based on our opinions and beliefs about ourselves which can be difficult to change. Your self-esteem can affect whether or not you like and value yourself as a person. We might also think of this as self-confidence.

There are 3 types of self-esteem:

- Overly high self-esteem - Feeling superior to others. People with overly high self-esteem are often arrogant and self-indulgent, and express feelings of entitlement
- Low self-esteem - Feeling inferior to others
- Healthy self-esteem - Having an honest and balanced self-view

The 3 C's of Self-esteem – If you want to be successful, focus on the three C's: **Competence, Confidence and Connection.** Whether you're at the beginning of your journey or ready to take your next bold step, you might have the same question that many people have: What can I do to become successful?

Tips to boost your self-esteem:

- Be kind to yourself
- Get to know yourself - what makes you happy and what do you value in life
- Try to challenge unkind thoughts about yourself
- Say positive things to yourself
- Practice saying no
- Try to avoid comparing yourself to others
- Do something nice for yourself

Self-Esteem Worksheet

When working on your self-esteem, it is important to reflect on your thoughts, actions, and accomplishments daily. Through this reflection you will learn more about yourself.

Directions: Rate how much you believe each statement from 0 to 10. "0" means you do not believe it at all and "10" means you completely believe it.

How do you truly feel about yourself?   **Rating**

1. I believe in myself   _____

2. I am just as valuable as other people   _____

3. I would rather be myself than someone else   _____

4. I am proud of my accomplishments   _____

5. I feel good when I get compliments   _____

6. I can handle criticism   _____

7. I am good at solving problems   _____

8. I love trying new things   _____

9. I respect myself   _____

10. I like the way I look   _____

11. I love myself even when others reject me   _____

12. I know my positive qualities   _____

13. I focus on my successes and not my failures   _____

14. I am not afraid to make mistakes   _____

15. I am happy to be me   _____

What do you need to change in order to move up one point on the rating scale?

Parent Approved _____ Teacher Approved_____ Total Points_____

Family Values

Family Values – morals/principles traditionally upheld and passed on within a family

Family values, sometimes referred to as familial morals, are traditional or cultural values that pertain to the family's structure, function, roles, beliefs, attitudes, and ideals. The concept of family values may also refer to the extent to which familial relationships are valued within people's lives.

Strong family values are the foundation of a happy and loving household. These shared ideas shape a family's structure, morals, priorities, and traditions. Many parents instill good family values in their children to help them develop into kind, responsible citizens. Families that align values typically have a stronger bond and more successful relationships. By contrast, a lack of family values can cause discord and dysfunction. What are family values, and how can you teach good values to your family?

10 Ingredients of Good Family Values

Honesty – sincerity, truthfulness

Integrity – the quality of being honest and having strong moral principles and moral uprightness

Respect - a feeling of deep admiration for someone or something based on their abilities, qualities, or achievements

Kindness – the quality of being friendly, generous and considerate

Love - an intense feeling of deep affection

Compassion – sympathetic pity and concern for the suffering or misfortunes of others

Faith - strong belief in God or in the doctrines of a religion based on scriptures

Humility - a modest or low view of one's own importance

Empathy - the ability to understand and share the feelings of another

Fairness – impartial and just treatment or behavior without favoritism or discrimination

Family Values Worksheet

Your values are the principles you believe are most important. Values help to determine your priorities in life and heavily influence decision-making. For example, a person who values wealth might prioritize their career, while a person who values family might try to spend more time at home. When people's actions do not align with their values, they can potentially become discontent.

Write down the first 3 words that come to mind when you think of your family.

1._____ 2._____ 3._____

Check which experiences you want more of in your family relationships.

Family Time____   One-on-One Time____   Family Outings____

Holiday Celebrations____   Vacations____   Religious Traditions____

On a scale of 1 (not well) to 10 (extremely well), please rate the following two questions:

How well do you communicate with your family? _____

How well does your family communicate with you? _____

What can you do to improve family dynamics? _____

Write True or False after each statement. {Each answer = 1 point}

Having values is important to me_____   All values are positive____   I love myself____

Different people have different values____   I get good grades____   I have good manners____

Values do not help us to make decisions ____   I finish my chores____   I make friends____

Spiritual affiliation is important____   I love money_____   I am popular with my friends____

Write down values you like _____ and/or dislike_____

Parent Approved _____   Teacher Approved_____   Total Points_____

Page 59

Education

Education-the act or process of imparting or acquiring knowledge (general or particular to a profession), developing the power of reasoning and judgment, and preparing oneself or others intellectually for a mature life

Why is it important to have a good education?

Learning nourishes the mind and allows you to grow. You can find new and exciting opportunities to advance your knowledge personally and professionally.

There are many advantages to obtaining a good education. Education is not just about getting a diploma; it is also important to develop literacy, thinking and problem-solving skills and positive character traits. Our community research team noted that early childhood education and youth development provide important health benefits.

Why is education more important than ever?

A good education is necessary to combat the decline in reading, writing and math skills, low test scores and low high school graduation rates that our society faces today. An education provides professional training for certain careers and often leads to financial stability. It also inspires innovation in our technologically advanced society and contributes to productivity.

What are other benefits of a good education?

Education helps a person to sharpen communication skills by learning to read, write, speak and listen. Education develops critical thinking skills which are vital in using logic when making decisions and interacting with others. Education expands the mind, embraces different experiences and perceptions, and works toward the betterment of all members of the global community. The following list includes additional benefits of a good education:

Valuable member of society – An education is believed to make someone a useful contributor to society.

Citizenship – Education can give people knowledge and skills to understand, challenge and engage in politics, media, civil society, economy and the law.

Financial security - Education can equip a person with the necessary knowledge and skills to make good financial decisions and secure their future.

Global impact - When considering major global challenges facing us today - climate change, hunger, poverty - education can help create a brighter future for humanity.

Strong values - Having an education can teach us about our place in this world and about our responsibility to humanity.

Confidence - Education is often considered a way to prove your knowledge and it can give you the confidence to express your opinions.

Economic growth - Education creates a talented workforce, with the skills and innovation needed to address pressing challenges and provide economic security with disposable income.

Critical thinking – Education helps develop critical thinking skills, organize learning, self-supervise and evaluate school tasks, which enhance future opportunities.

Goals – Education helps students realize their interests and help them find realistic paths to approaching their life goals.

Volunteers – Education provides opportunities to volunteer and increase awareness of others' needs. In turn, this will help students become competent, employable and better meet their learning objectives.

Independence - Education encourages independence as it teaches you to be a self-starter, interact with new people, try new things, study by yourself, and take ownership of your time and what you choose to do with it.

Stability - Education, especially a college degree, can increase your chances for better career opportunities and open new doors for yourself which can lead to stability.

Academic Worksheet

Directions: Use the SMART goals guide below to help plan your goals. Write your goals at the top of the staircase and the steps you need to take to achieve them. Each answer = 1 point.

S.M.A.R.T. - Specific, Measurable, Achievable, Relevant, and Time-Bound

Do you like school? Yes ___ or No ____ Why or why not? _____

_____

What school do you attend? _____

What grade? ____ What's your favorite subject? _____

English ___   Math ___   Science ___   History ___   Physical Education ___

Computer ___   Language ___   Religion ___   What's your grade average? A, B, C, D, F ___

What do you want to be in life? _____

Do you want to go to college? Yes___ or No ___ Why or why not? _____

How to reach my goals? Maintain ___ or Improve ___ my behavior
How to reach my goals? Maintain ___ or Improve ___ my grades

Directions: Set your target, plan your action and achieve your goal. Write your goal at the top of the staircase and the steps you need to take to achieve it. {Each answer = 1 point}

	My Goal
Step 2	
Step 1	

Parent Approved _____ Teacher Approved_____ Total Points_____

Health & Fitness

Health & Fitness- the ability to perform physical work, training, and other activities

Fitness involves activity of some sort that stimulates various parts of the body and maintains a certain condition within the body. **Health**, on the other hand, involves every system of a body and is achieved through a lifestyle that supports health.

Why are health and fitness important in life?

Frequent and regular physical exercise boosts the immune system and helps prevent heart disease, cardiovascular disease, Type 2 diabetes, mellitus, and obesity. Nutrition is the provision of materials (in the form of food) necessary for cells and organisms to support life.

Why are health and fitness goals important?

Fitness goals are an essential part of your wellness journey. By setting goals, you are able to hold yourself accountable, show what you are capable of, and push through the more difficult moments to make a longer-lasting charge.

What are factors in achieving health and fitness?

There are five components of physical fitness: 1. Body composition, 2. Flexibility, 3. Muscular strength, 4. Muscular endurance, and 5. Cardiorespiratory endurance. A well-balanced exercise program should include activities that address all of the health-related components of fitness.

What are 3 factors affecting fitness?

Three key things that healthy people do every day are exercise, maintain a nutritious diet and get a good night's sleep.

Health & Fitness Worksheet

Exercise is good for you no matter how old you are. It reduces your risk of getting many diseases, such as cancer, heart disease, and diabetes. It also reduces stress, helps you sleep better, and improves mental health. Here are some questions about your lifestyle and tips for incorporating exercise into your life at any age.

FOOD FOR THOUGHT

1. What is your physical health condition? Good _____   Fair_____   Poor_____

2. Are you in good physical shape? _____ Overweight? _____   On a diet? _____

3. Do you eat 3 meals per day?_____

4. What is your favorite junk food?_____ How often do you eat junk food?_____

5. Do you eat a lot of fruits and vegetables? _____   Do you take vitamins?_____

6. How many sodas do you drink daily? None_____   Very little_____   Too many_____

7. Do you drink enough water?_____

8. How much water should you drink per day?   4 cups_____   6 cups_____   8 cups _____

GET YOURSELF FIT

9. Do you have a lot of stress?_____ Do you play physical games?_____

Do you like to exercise?____ How often do you exercise?_____

10. What is your favorite sport to watch?_____ Do you play any sports? _____ If yes, which sports? _____

11. Do you take naps?_____   Do you get 8 hours of sleep per night? _____

THINGS YOU CAN TRY TO DO

Ditch TV, go out and play, ride a bike, roller or ice skate, skateboard, plant a garden _____

Getting in shape can be easy. Choose a workout space, set a schedule, set some goals.

50 Jumping Jacks - 25 Pushups – 15 Arm Rotations - 40 Sit-Ups – 50 Squats – 20 Minute Run

Parent Approved _____ Teacher Approved_____ Total Points_____

Nutrition

Nutrition is the process of taking in food and converting it into energy and other vital nutrients required for life. In the process, organisms utilize nutrients. The main nutrients are carbohydrates, fats, proteins, vitamins, minerals, and roughage.

What is nutrition in our life? Nutrition is a critical part of health and development. Better nutrition is related to improved infant, child and maternal health, stronger immune systems, safer pregnancy and childbirth, lower risk of non-communicable diseases (such as diabetes and cardiovascular disease), and longevity.

What is the role of nutrition in our body? Nutrition has one or more of these basic functions: provides energy, contributes to body structure, and/or regulates chemical processes in the body. These functions allow us to detect and respond to environmental surroundings, move, excrete waste, respire (breathe), grow, and reproduce.

What is the most important nutrient in nutrition? Water is the most essential nutrient. A person can only survive a few days without consuming water.

Nutrition Worksheet

Nutrition - the process of providing or obtaining food necessary for health and growth

List foods that contain these important nutrients

Vitamin A increases resistance to infection and improves eyesight

_____

Vitamin B aids in good digestion and steady nerves

_____

Vitamin C prevents scurvy and helps our muscles and gums

_____

Vitamin D increases resistance to infection and improves eyesight

_____

Carbohydrates give us strength and energy

Fats, in limited amounts, enhance our skin and give us energy

Proteins build and repair our bodies

Teamwork/Sportsmanship

Teamwork and Sportsmanship – Teamwork in sports helps children learn the art of willingness to have self-control. Sportsmanship teaches children to be respectful and to have a positive attitude. Learning equality and patience will teach our children to respect everyone on the team.

Teamwork

Teamwork – collaborative effort of a group to achieve a common goal or complete a task in an effective, efficient way.

What are the benefits of teamwork?

Research shows that collaborative problem-solving leads to better outcomes. People are more likely to take risks and innovate if they have the support of a team. Working in a team encourages personal growth, increases job satisfaction, and reduces stress.

Teamwork:
- cultivates effective communication
- improves brainstorming
- encourages a common goal
- enhances problem solving skills
- helps build trust
- improves company culture
- creates efficiency

Sportsmanship

Sportsmanship - when people who are playing or watching a sport treat each other with respect. This includes players, parents, coaches, officials and fans.

.

What are examples of good sportsmanship?

Examples include shaking hands (before and after a game), honesty, kindness, responsibility, respect, and sympathy. Each of these examples is taught early and often across all sports.

What are characteristics of sportsmanship?

- If you lose, don't make excuses
- If you win, don't rub it in
- Learn from mistakes and get back in the game
- Always do your best
- If someone makes a mistake, remain encouraging and avoid criticizing.
- Show respect for yourself, your family, your team, and officials of the game

What is poor sportsmanship?

Examples include verbal abuse or taunting of an opponent or game official, an excessive celebration following a significant play, or feigning injury.

What are five main qualities of true sportsmanship?

Qualities of an ideal sportsman are determination, optimization, stamina, perseverance, and decisiveness. A true sportsman should have these qualities before playing any game.

Sportsmanship

Sportsmanship is a sign of honor in sports. It involves the conduct of players, spectators, coaches, and school authorities as courteous, fair and respectful.

Sportsmanship Worksheet

Emotions are high during any competitive event. You could experience either the joy of winning or disappointment of losing. The way that you handle winning or losing can impact how other people feel about you after the competition. Regardless of the outcome, you can still use good social skills to keep from being a boastful winner or sore loser.

Directions: Sportsmanship is when you follow the rules and are kind and respectful to others whether you win or lose. Check True or False on the lines below.

- Shake hands with the other team even if you lose. __ True __ False
- Congratulate others when they do a good job. __ True __ False
- Be honest and do not cheat. __ True __ False
- Be kind and do not taunt or call names. __ True __ False
- Keep a positive attitude at all times. __ True __ False
- Do not brag if you win a competition. __ True __ False
- Understand how other people feel if they lose. __ True __ False
- Use coping skills if you get angry during a game. __ True __ False
- Give positive feedback to your teammates. __ True __ False
- Listen to feedback from others without getting upset. __ True __ False
- Accept the results of a game. __ True __ False
- Show respect and concern to anyone who gets injured. __ True __ False
- Do not quit or give up if you're losing a game. __ True __ False

A good winner or loser is someone who accepts the outcome of a competition. This is called being a good sport. Write down other behaviors a good sport can display.

_____

Parent Approved _____ Teacher Approved _____ Total Points_____

Work Ethic

Work Ethic – a set of principles that guide a person's behavior with a commitment to perform a job to the best of their ability

A strong work ethic means that people take enough satisfaction in their job to complete every task and prioritize their work/life balance. People with a strong work ethic take pride in their job and view every task as important.

Ten traits of a strong work ethic:

Appearance, Attendance, Attitude, Character, Communication, Cooperation, Organizational Skills, Productivity, Respect and Teamwork are defined as essential for student success. Each of these traits is described below.

1. Appearance: Displays proper dress, grooming, hygiene and manners

2. Attendance: Attends class, arrives and leaves on time, notifies instructor of upcoming absence in advance and makes up assignments promptly

3. Attitude: Thinks positively, appears confident and has true hope of self

4. Character: Displays loyalty, honesty, dependability, reliability, initiative and self-control

5. Communication: Displays proper verbal and non-verbal skills and listens

6. Cooperation: Displays leadership skills, properly handles criticism, conflicts, and stress, maintains proper relationships with peers and follows chain of command

7. Organizational Skills: Demonstrates skills in managing people, prioritizing and dealing with change

8. Productivity: Follows safety practices, conserves resources and follows instructions

9. Respect: Shows understanding and tolerance, deals properly with differences

10. Teamwork: Respects rights of others, is helpful and confident, displays a customer service attitude and seeks continuous learning

Work Ethic Worksheet

Work Ethic is pitching in to help and working hard to get a job done. It is not being lazy. There are many ways to show a good work ethic.

Directions: Answer each of the questions below.

A. What chores and responsibilities do you have at your home and school?

_____

1. What is work ethic?

- o The way a person approaches their work
- o The way a person delegates their work to other people
- o The way a person tries to avoid difficult projects
- o The way a person looks for a job

2. What is a challenge that can result from a poor work ethic?

- o Difficulty finding a new job
- o Increased responsibility
- o Getting promoted beyond your ability
- o Jealousy from a co-worker

3. What is dependability?

- o Demonstrating that people can count on and trust you
- o Giving up easily when a project becomes challenging
- o Being humble and recognizing others
- o Making promises you don't keep

4. Work Ethic Tips

Show up regularly, Arrive on time and ready to work, Listen to and follow instructions, Be willing to learn, Perform quality work, Display a positive can-do attitude, Complete work in a timely fashion

Parent Approved_____ **Teacher Approved**_____ **Total Points**_____

Page 73

Recreation

Recreation – a way of enjoying yourself when you are not working

Recreation refers to those activities that people choose to do to refresh their bodies and minds and make their leisure time more interesting and enjoyable. Examples of recreational activities are walking, swimming, meditating, reading, playing games and dancing.

What does recreation mean in life? Recreation includes leisure activities chosen by an individual for the purpose of improving their life. These activities are of a constructive nature. They are time-using and not time-consuming. They are healthy - physically, mentally and socially.

There are 2 categories of recreational activities:

Recreational opportunities fall into two broad categories: active recreation and passive recreation. Active recreation refers to a structured individual or team activity that requires physical effort and the use of special facilities, courses, fields or equipment. Examples include dancing, swimming, hiking or cycling. Passive recreation involves noncompetitive and low-impact activities such as listening to music, reading and watching television.

There are 3 types of recreational activities:

- **Physical activities** (sports, games, fitness)
- **Social activities** (parties, picnics, book clubs)
- **Exciting activities** (amusement parks, camping, rafting)

What is the main objective of recreational activities?

Recreational activity relieves feelings of fatigue, restores energy and promotes a sense of joy. Without recreation, life would be uninteresting and unhealthy.

Recreation Worksheet

Recreation is a leisure activity that we do in our free time or for fun. It is what we do when not going to class, working, sleeping or taking care of responsibilities.

1. Do you have a lot of free time?

2. What do you like to do in your free time?

Now, read the sentences below. On a scale of 1 to 4, rate how much you believe each statement. "0" means you do not believe it and "4" means you completely believe it. Then, compare your and your classmates' answers.

- Computer games are fun. 0   1   2   3   4
- Everyone should take a two-hour nap in the afternoon. 0   1   2   3   4
- People can't really enjoy free time if they don't have much money.
  0 1 2 3 4
- Swimming is dangerous. 0   1   2   3   4
- Walking is the best form of exercise. 0   1   2   3   4
- Reading is the best way to spend free time because it can make you smarter.
  0 1 2 3 4
- Watching TV is a waste of time. 0   1   2   3   4
- Everyone should have a hobby. 0   1   2   3   4
- Exercising or playing sports is the best way to spend free time because it can make you healthier. 0   1   2   3   4
- Surfing the internet makes people more intelligent. 0   1   2   3   4
- Going for a drive is boring. 0   1   2   3   4
- Most people have a lot of free time. 0   1   2   3   4

Parent Approved_____ Teacher Approved_____ Total Points_____

Community Service

Community Service – volunteer work intended to help people in a particular area

Community Service is when you do something for someone else without the intention or expectation of getting a reward or money. This service should benefit someone other than yourself and it should be done because you want to help and not because you are required to do so.

Why is community service important? Unpaid volunteers are often the glue that holds a community together. Volunteering allows you to connect with your community and make it a better place to live. Helping out with even the smallest tasks can make a real difference in the lives of people, animals and organizations in need.

What are examples of community service? Examples include cleaning your neighborhood, helping sick kids or the elderly, promoting animal welfare, tutoring in reading, writing, math or other subjects, assisting at a homeless shelter and cooking. We have put together a list of community service project ideas that cover all these areas and more.

Volunteers can:

- Give you a sense of achievement and purpose
- Inspire you to feel part of a community
- Help you feel better about yourself by improving your self-esteem and confidence
- Encourage you to share your talents, learn new skills and create a better work-life balance
- Raise awareness to important issues or causes

Helping people can change your life!

Community Service Worksheet

What is Community Service?

Community service is volunteering to help those in your community. It might be an activity that is done once or on a regular basis for an individual or organization. It is often referred to as "giving back to your community." Volunteering without pay, whether it is to help the less fortunate or to clean up your neighborhood, is the essence of community service.

Types of Community Service

Soup Kitchen   Homeless Shelter   Food Pantry   Visiting the Elderly

Animal Shelter   Mentoring   Tutoring

Directions: Please answer the questions below.

Do you prefer to work indoors or outdoors? _____

Do you prefer to work with people or animals? _____

Do you prefer to work in a group or alone? _____

Why do you think community service is important? _____

_____

My community service project will be _____

_____

I chose this because _____

My goals are _____

_____

Parent Approved_____ Teacher Approved_____ Total Points_____

Teen Time Management

Time management is the art of effectively planning your time to efficiently and productively complete activities and tasks in the appropriate amount of time. Time management also involves prioritizing your to-do list so that you complete tasks in order of importance.

What is time management? Time management is the process of organizing and planning how to allocate time between different tasks and activities. It allows you to work smarter, not harder, and leads to greater productivity and reduced stress.

What are benefits of good time management?

Time management isn't just about getting work done. It's also about ensuring that you put yourself and your mental well-being first. Consistently including time for yourself in your schedule helps to keep your mental health and life in balance.

What are 4 types of time management? The Early Bird, the Multitasker, The Helper, and The Deliberator. Each of these personalities has their own benefits and drawbacks, and knowing your time-management personality can help you choose the best strategies that work for you.

What are 5 key elements of time management?

- Set reminders for all your tasks. The key to success in time management is to know your deadlines and set reminders...
- Create a daily planner
- Give each task a time limit
- Block out distractions
- Establish a routine

What are the 4 P's of time management?

The 4 P's of time management are Planning, Prioritization, Performance and Personalization. Planning sets a roadmap, prioritizing focuses on key tasks, performance enhances efficiency, and personalization adapts strategies to individual styles.

The 4 D's of Management Skills

Placing a task or project into one of these categories helps you manage your limited time more effectively and stay focused on what matters most to you.

- Do: Perform Immediate Actions. The first 'D' encourages undertaking tasks that are urgent, essential, and require immediate attention. ...
- Delegate: Assign Responsibility to Others. ...
- Defer: Postpone Non-urgent Tasks. ..
- Delete: Eliminate Unnecessary Tasks.

Time Management

"Your future is created by what you do today, not tomorrow."

Robert Kiyosaki

"Time isn't the main thing. It's the only thing."

Miles Davis

Time Management Worksheet

Estimate the amount of time you spend in these activities during a 7-day week.

SCHOOL	TOTAL WEEKLY HOURS
In class (e.g., 5 days/week x 7 hours/day = 35 hours/week)	
Homework: Subject 1_____	_____
Homework: Subject 2_____	_____
Homework: Subject 3_____	_____
Homework: Subject 4_____	_____
Homework: Subject 5_____	_____
Homework: Subject 6_____	_____
Homework: Subject 7_____	_____

EXTRACURRICULARS	TOTAL WEEKLY HOURS
Paid Job_____	_____
Community Service_____	_____
Sports, Visual & Performing Arts_____	_____
Other (e.g., SAT prep)_____	_____

UNSTRUCTURED TIME	TOTAL WEEKLY HOURS
Playtime, Downtime, Family Time_____	_____
Necessities (e.g., grooming, eating, transportation)_____	_____
Chores_____	_____

School_____+ Extracurricular_____+ Unstructured_____ = Weekly Total_____

Making Cents
Teen Money Management

Money management is learning how to earn, save, spend, borrow and repay money responsibly. Preteens and teenagers learn how to manage money by watching how adults handle money. Giving preteens and teenagers more responsibility for their own money helps them learn lifelong money management skills.

What are basic money skills? The first step into the world of money is education. Income, budget, savings, investments, bank account, interest, credit and debt are pillars that support most of the financial decisions we'll make in our lives.

Why is it important for teens to manage their money? Teens must learn that money is earned and does not come easily. A solid understanding of money will help them make better financial decisions in life. Teaching teens about saving money and budgeting will help them minimize debt and avoid financial problems.

What are 4 principles of money management? It is important to understand the four principles of finance: income, savings, expenses and investments. Following these principles can help maintain finances at a healthy level.

How does the 50/30/20 rule work? One of the most common types of percentage-based budgets is the 50/30/20 rule. The idea is to divide your income into three categories: 50% needs, 30% wants and 20% savings.

What is the golden rule of money management? The golden rule is: Don't spend more than you earn.

Budget Worksheet

NAME_____   MONTH _____

SAVINGS GOAL_____

INCOME/ALLOWANCE/GIFT	AMOUNT
TOTAL INCOME	

EXPENSES	AMOUNT
TOTAL EXPENSES	

SAVINGS GOAL	
AMOUNT IN SAVINGS	

Cooking Skills for Preteens

If you're a preteen at home, it's important to start cooking at an early age, with parental supervision, preferably at the age of six. Sound crazy? While it may try your parent's patience at times, cooking with preteens has loads of benefits that carry way beyond the kitchen. Cooking helps build self-esteem, teaches the importance of following directions and (hopefully) puts kids on a path to healthier eating habits. Plus, involvement in choosing and preparing meals can be a powerful tool in overcoming picky eating - something parents may face at some point.

There's no specific age at which preteens should start cooking, as readiness varies from person to person. However, introducing cooking skills to preteens can be a valuable life skill with many benefits.

Cooking can help young people learn and practice basic math concepts and build language skills. Creating meals can help build self-confidence and lay the foundation for healthy eating habits. It may take a little extra time and some simple prep work, but the results will pay off.

Is cooking a necessary skill? Even if you never cooked anything other than a grilled cheese sandwich, expanding your cooking skills can improve your quality of life. Cooking is a great skill that also increases knowledge of different cuisines and flavors around the world.

What are benefits of cooking?
- Acquire a new skill
- Become more independent
- Reduce intake of highly processed foods
- Control the amount of sauces and seasonings
- Make foods that you and your family enjoy
- Save money by eating out less often
- Choose healthy ingredients like fruits, vegetables and protein foods

Kitchen Safety Worksheet

Cooking can be fun, but your kitchen can be a dangerous place. You are more likely to get injured or sick in the kitchen than in any other room in your house.

Each item below can cause injuries. Can you identify each one?

STOVE	TOASTER	KNIFE	SPONGE	GRATER	GLASS	BLENDER

Below are common accidents that can happen in the kitchen. Please choose items from the above list to fill in the blanks.

➤ Burn - when a part of your body is injured as a result of touching something hot. List items in your kitchen that can cause a burn.

_____   _____   _____

➤ Cut – an open incision or wound made with a sharp-edged tool or object. List kitchen items that can cause a cut.

_____   _____   _____

➤ Fall – moving downward to the ground without any control. List items in your kitchen that could cause you to fall.

_____   _____   _____

➤ Bacteria - tiny organisms that live on food and in unsanitary areas in the kitchen. Name some items in your kitchen that could harbor bacteria:

_____   _____   _____

Choose words from the list below to fill in the sentences on preventing kitchen accidents.

1. Always use an _____ when removing hot items from the oven.
2. Make sure your smoke_____ is working.
3. Know how to use your _____ so you do not cut yourself.
4. Clean up _____ quickly to prevent slipping and falling.
5. Wear _____ and safe clothing while cooking.
6. Wash your _____ after touching raw meats to prevent the spread of bacteria.
7. Have a _____extinguisher handy to put out any kitchen fires

SHOES	DETECTOR	FIRE	SPILLS	HANDS	OVEN MITT	KNIVES

"No one is born a great cook, one learns by doing."

Julia Child

"The secret of good cooking is, first, having a love of it."

James Beard

Cooking Skills Worksheet

Preteens can usually work independently in the kitchen. However, before they work on their own, they should have close adult supervision to assess whether they can follow basic rules such as tucking pan handles, unplugging electrical appliances and using a chef's knife safely. Cooking can be fun, but your kitchen can be a dangerous place. You are more likely to get injured or sick in the kitchen than in any other room in your house.

Please place a checkmark by the tasks or foods you know how to do/make.

CLEANING APPLIANCES

How to Wash, Rinse and Sanitize Equipment_____

COOKING SAFETY

Wash hands_____ Clean as you go____ Knife safety____ Wipe spills immediately____

COOKING METHODS

Boiling ____ Frying ____ Baking ____ Steaming ____ Grilling ____ Roasting ____

BREAKFAST

Hot cereal____ Boiled eggs____ Scrambled eggs____ Sausage____ Bacon____

Toast____ Pancakes____ French toast____

LUNCH

Grilled cheese _____ Steamed hot dog_____ Pan fried hamburger_____

DINNER

Rice____ Pasta____ Baked or mashed potato____ Baked or fried cheese____

Broiled steak or chops _____

Household Chores

Chores are important because they help young people learn how to care for themselves, their home and family. They develop important organizational skills and learn responsibility and self-reliance.

1. Chores teach life skills – You're young now, but you won't be a kid forever! Cooking, doing laundry and budgeting are just a few skills you will need once you move out on your own. Not all schools teach life skills so learning at home is even more important.

2. Chores help kids learn responsibility and self-reliance - Assigning chores to children helps teach them responsibility. Personal tasks, such as cleaning their room or doing laundry, can help them become more self-reliant. Children may also take pride in being mature enough to take care of themselves.

3. Chores teach teamwork – Learning to be a productive member of a team can be modeled for young people through housework. Members of your family "team" are accountable to each other, and there are consequences when you don't meet each other's expectations. Learning these lessons at home, where mistakes are more easily forgiven, can help kids develop strong teamwork skills to use at school or work.

4. Chores reinforce respect – It takes moving away from home for most of us to fully appreciate all the hard work people do around the house. Kids are no different, but assigning chores may help this insight come a little quicker. Kids may become aware of the messes they make if they're tasked with cleaning up around the house, and gain more respect of the work that goes into maintaining a home.

5. Chores build a strong work ethic – This trait is highly valued by many people so why not instill a strong work ethic at a young age? Chores are commonly tied to a reward, such as an allowance or TV time. Paying children for a job well done can also spark an entrepreneurial spirit and inspire them to work outside the home once they reach their teen and adult years.

6. Chores improve planning and time management skills – Sometimes there are so many things to do in a day, and fitting them all into our daily lives is a challenge. Chores can help kids build good time management skills early. Juggling schoolwork deadlines, housework and social lives helps them learn to set priorities and manage their time. These are important skills to have before entering the workforce.

7. Chores give families a chance to bond - People often lament that chores take up time they could spend with their kids or grandkids. Chores can actually create special moments between children and adults. Little ones who always want to help will feel important and receive a self-esteem boost, and moody teens may decide to open up over a shared task.

Chores for Preteens
- Put away their belongings
- Help to prepare meals
- Do the laundry
- Fold and put away clean clothes
- Tidy up their room
- Pack their school lunch
- Dust, vacuum, sweep and mop floors
- Set and clear the table
- Wash and put away the dishes
- Mow the lawn
- Feed, walk family pets, clean animal cages and litter boxes
- Take out the garbage and recyclables
- Wash the car

"Our children won't become responsible unless they have responsibility. And like everything else, that starts in the home."

Thomas Lickona, Ph.D.

Preteen Household Chores Worksheet

Name_____ Week of_____

CHORE	SUN	MON	TUE	WED	THUR	FRI	SAT
Make Bed							
Make Breakfast							
Wash/dry dishes							
Load/unload dishwasher							
Wipe down kitchen counter							
Help with dinner prep							
Set/clear dinner table							
Empty & put away backpack							
Prepare & pack lunch							
Put away clothes							
Tidy bedroom							
Tidy living room/family room							
Feed pets/walk dog							
Check mail							
Wash car							
Rake leaves/cut grass							

Congratulations Tool-Mate!

Once you complete all the lesson plans in The Tooliez Tool-Rific Workbook, please review the material with a parent, guardian, teacher or counselor.

Parent/Guardian: _____

Teacher/Counselor:_____

Tool-Mate:_____ Date____

Order your Certificate Online Today!

www.tooliezworld.com

Tool-Rific Kid Tips

Dream Big, Make Plans, Believe in Yourself, Study Hard, Work Smart, Stay Focused, Meet your Goals!

To succeed in life, prioritize (1) Faith in God, (2) A Good Education, and (3) Your Career. A serious relationship will follow.

If you associate with people who have no motivation or ambition and who are not doing anything positive, guess who will follow in their footsteps? **YOU!**

If you associate with people who are motivated and ambitious and do positive things, guess who will follow in their footsteps? **YOU!**

When you leave home, always remember that you represent God, yourself, your family and your culture.

1. Create a vision board with short and long-term goals

2. Do not allow yourself to be idle; keep busy and limit time on social media

3. Focus on self-improvement by becoming spiritually guided, bonding with your family, and connecting and socializing with family and friends

4. Participate in sports, clubs and arts

If it doesn't make you Better, Smarter, Faster or Stronger, Leave it alone.

Journal Time

Keeping a journal is simply writing down your thoughts and feelings to express yourself and reflect on your experiences. If you struggle with stress, depression or anxiety, writing in a journal can help you gain control of your emotions and improve your mental health.

_____

_____

_____

_____

_____

_____

_____

_____

_____

_____

_____

Journal Time

_____

_____

_____

_____

_____

_____

_____

_____

_____

_____

_____

_____

_____

Journal Time

Journal Time

_____

_____

_____

_____

_____

_____

_____

_____

_____

_____

_____

_____

_____

Journal Time

_____

_____

_____

_____

_____

_____

_____

_____

_____

_____

_____

_____

Journal Time

_____

_____

_____

_____

_____

_____

_____

_____

_____

_____

_____

_____

_____

Journal Time

_____

_____

_____

_____

_____

_____

_____

_____

_____

_____

_____

_____

_____

_____

www.ingramcontent.com/pod-product-compliance
Lightning Source LLC
LaVergne TN
LVHW070841080426
835513LV00024B/2425